ISBN 978-0-331-39821-2
PIBN 11118169

This book is a reproduction of an important historical work. Forgotten Books uses
state-of-the-art technology to digitally reconstruct the work, preserving the original format
whilst repairing imperfections present in the aged copy. In rare cases, an imperfection in
the original, such as a blemish or missing page, may be replicated in our edition. We do,
however, repair the vast majority of imperfections successfully; any imperfections that
remain are intentionally left to preserve the state of such historical works.

NORMALIZED PRICES FOR RESOURCE PLANNING: A COMPARISON OF ALTERNATIVES

Robert D. Niehaus

U.S. Department of Agriculture

Economics, Statistics, and Cooperatives Service

ESCS-39

BIBLIOGRAPHIC DATA SHEET	1. Report No. ESCS-39	2.	3. Recipient's Accession No.

4. Title and Subtitle	5. Report Date
NORMALIZED PRICES FOR RESOURCE PLANNING: A COMPARISON OF ALTERNATIVES	November 1978
	6.

7. Author(s) Robert D. Niehaus	8. Performing Organization Rept. No. ESCS-39

9. Performing Organization Name and Address Natural Resource Economics Division Economics, Statistics, and Cooperatives Service U.S. Department of Agriculture Washington, D.C. 20250	10. Project/Task/Work Unit No.
	11. Contract/Grant No.

12. Sponsoring Organization Name and Address	13. Type of Report & Period Covered Final--1976
	14.

15. Supplementary Notes

16. Abstracts

Normalized prices are estimated prices used to forecast water and related land resource returns. This report examines the characteristics of normalized prices issued periodically by the U.S. Water Resources Council. This study also evaluates several alternative procedures--trend analysis, weighted average techniques, and a structural approach--for calculating normalized prices. These techniques should be of particular interest to analysts and planners in public agencies of all levels of government.

17. Key Words and Document Analysis. 17a. Descriptors

Computation
Economic analysis
Estimates
Evaluation
Forecasting
Government policies
Land
Normalizing
Planning
Prices

Resources
Structural analysis
Variability
Water

17b. Identifiers/Open-Ended Terms
Agricultural markets
Market conditions
Normalized prices
Structural models
Trend analysis
U.S. Water Resources Council
Weighted average

17c. COSATI Field Group   02-B, 05-C, 08-H

22. Current NTIS prices
Paper: $ 4.50
Fiche: $ 3.00
NTIS prices subject to change.
NTIS price codes will be A 03
for paper and A 01 for fiche.

18 Availability Statement Available from: NATIONAL TECHNICAL INFORMATION SERVICE, 5285 Port Royal Rd., Springfield, VA 22161	19. Security Class (This Report) UNCLASSIFIED	21. No. of Pages 28
	20. Security Class (This Page) UNCLASSIFIED	22. Price See above

FORM NTIS-35 (REV. 10-73)   ENDORSED BY ANSI AND UNESCO   THIS FORM MAY BE REPRODUCED   USCOMM-DC 8265-P74

CONTENTS

About the Author

The author, Robert D. Niehaus, is presently the
staff economist for the Northeast-Midwest Insti-
tute, Washington, D.C. At the time this report
was written, he was an economist with the Natural Resource Economics Division, Economics,
Statistics, and Cooperatives Service, U.S. Department of Agriculture.

Washington, D.C. 20250   November 1978

SUMMARY

Normalized prices are the prices observed if the market conditions had been normal.
Normalized prices are a specific kind of shadow price, reflecting expected net returns of Government projects and resource plans to the public.

The trend analysis and modified trend approach, using dummy variables, have been used
in the past for calculating normalized prices. Both of these techniques, however,
have no theoretical basis and yield unsatisfactory results when large price fluctuations occur. An alternative is to use weighted averages of past prices, which guaran-
tees that normalized prices will be dampened images of actual prices. A model of
price-normalizing behavior suggests that the weights should be higher for more recent
prices and lower for earlier prices. The weights can be estimated statistically.
This approach is currently used by the U.S. Water Resources Council.

The final alternative considered uses structural models of agricultural markets.
Theoretically the most satisfactory, this approach provides an explicit framework for
incorporating relevant information about supply, demand, and Government policy conditions in agricultural markets. Further research on the structural approach is recom-
mended.

NORMALIZED PRICES FOR RESOURCE PLANNING: A COMPARISON OF ALTERNATIVES

By

Robert D. Niehaus
Economist

INTRODUCTION

The U.S. Water Resources Council (WRC) is an independent executive agency of the
Federal Government. It consists of the heads of several executive departments and
agencies and the regional river basin commissions. WRC coordinates the conservation,
development, and use of water and related land resources in the United States.

WRC administers a unified policy on prices to be used for planning purposes. The basis of this policy is articulated in the Principles for Planning Water and Land Resources 1/ and Standards for Planning Water and Related Land Resources 2/ (referred to
in this report as Principles and Standards). In essence, the basic policy calls for
the use of current actual prices of all goods and services in estimating the potential
costs and benefits of a public natural resource plan.

The WRC has found it necessary to treat prices in the agricultural sector as exceptions to the basic pricing policy established in the Principles and Standards. Instead
of using current actual prices of food and fiber products and inputs to evaluate the
agricultural effects of plans, planners use "current normalized" prices published an-
nually by the WRC. 3/

The normalized prices published by the WRC are potentially significant determinants of
the economic viability of many Government projects. They also affect the allocation
of project costs between private individuals and public agencies. These prices can
therefore influence the extent of public activity in the U.S. agricultural sector. For
this reason, it is important to take a close look at WRC's pricing policy. This report
will concentrate on two essential features of this policy--what normalized prices are
and how they may be calculated. In the discussion that follows, normalized prices will
be analyzed as specific types of shadow prices, and criteria will be presented that
give reasons for using the normalized price system. Attention will then be directed to
alternative techniques for calculating normalized prices and to comparing these alternatives.

1/ Water Resources Council, Principles for Planning Water and Land Resources,
Washington, D.C., 1970.
2/ Water Resources Council, Standards for Planning Water and Land Resources,
Washington, D.C., 1970.
3/ Water Resources Council, Agricultural Price Standards, Washington, D.C.,
Oct. 1976.

ACTUAL, NORMALIZED, AND SHADOW PRICES

The economic evaluation of public projects requires a set of product and resource prices to be used in calculating expected net returns from the project. These prices are frequently called shadow prices, and they play an important role in determining whether or not a project is economically viable. They are a measure of social value of the goods and resources used in association with the project.4/

The shadow price concept encompasses a number of specific meanings but can be sorted into two categories. First and in a positive case, shadow prices may be estimates of actual prices expected to prevail over a project's lifetime. The project analyst forecasts, with as much accuracy as possible, the prices of the goods and services relevant for the project under consideration.

Second, shadow prices may be normative. Normative price estimates prevail when agricultural marketing conditions differ from the actual or from a likelihood over which a project exists. These conditions reflect value judgments, as would be the case if a project benefitting primarily poor people was evaluated by one set of shadow prices and another set was applied to a project benefitting primarily wealthy people. Conversely, these shadow prices may reflect efficiency considerations as in the case of shadow prices chosen to compensate for monopoly, Government price supports, or variable weather.

These two kinds of shadow prices are identical under conditions of full employment, longrun market equilibrium, and perfect competition. To the degree that these conditions are fulfilled, actual prices of goods and resources accurately measure their marginal value to consumers and producers. To the extent that these conditions are not met, actual prices poorly indicate the contribution of goods or resources to total welfare. The normative shadow price concept then becomes relevant.

In the United States, an important application of the shadow pricing concept is in planning for water and related land resources. The basic pricing policy in this area, established by the WRC, is that:·

> . . . relative price relationships and the general level of
> prices prevailing during the planning study will be assumed
> to hold generally for the future, except where specific
> studies and considerations indicate otherwise.5/

Under the guidelines set forth by the WRC, the shadow prices used to evaluate water and related land resource plans will be the actual prices prevailing at the time of evaluation. The WRC uses, in terms of the shadow price categories, the first or positive type of prices that corresponds as closely to actual prices as possible.

4/ This report will not survey the literature on shadow pricing. However, the interested reader should refer to A. R. Prest and R. Turvey, "Cost-Benefit Analysis: A Survey," Surveys of Economic Theory, Vol. III, American Economic Association and Royal Economic Society, New York: St. Martin's Press, 1966, pp. 162 ff.; E. J. Mishan, Cost-Benefit Analysis: An Introduction, New York: Praeger, 1971, pp.79-89; S. A. Marglin, Public Investment Criteria, Cambridge: MIT Press, 1967, pp. 40-92; and J. P. Gittinger, Economic Analysis of Agricultural Projects, Baltimore: The Johns Hopkins University Press, 1972, pp. 31-46. For an analysis based on the correspondence between the shadow prices of a mathematical program and shadow pricing for resource planning, see F. J. Stewart and R. A. Greenhalgh, "The Use of Shadow Prices in Determining Potential for Natural Resource Development Programs," Economic Report 90, Food and Resource Economic Division, University of Florida, Gainesville, Florida, processed, Jan. 1977.
  5/ Water Resources Council, Principles for Planning, pp. 10-11.

The special feature of the WRC price policy is that, instead of forecasting actual prices, it assumes that future actual prices will be the same as current actual prices. This approach gives rise to prediction errors, but the use of forecasted prices will also result in errors.

It should be noted that this official pricing policy excludes the consideration of efficiency and distributional questions in choosing appropriate shadow prices. Some of these issues, relating to environmental quality and the distribution of income, are addressed in the Principles and Standards, but are treated in a nonprice framework.

In plans affecting the agricultural sector, the WRC recognizes several exceptions to its basic guidelines. One exception toward shadow pricing concerns the plans that affect agricultural production enough to have an impact on commodity prices. In this case, the change in consumer's surplus, resulting from the project, is estimated by using a price that is midway between the price expected without the plan and the price expected with the plan. This exception, while deviating from the use of current prices, nevertheless focuses on actual prices that are likely to prevail with and without the plan. This is clearly a positive interpretation of the shadow price concept.

Other exceptions recognized under current policy permit the consideration of certain efficiency questions in calculating agricultural shadow prices. These exceptions put the WRC's agricultural shadow prices into the normative category described above. Specifically, these prices are estimates of what current prices would be if market influences were normal. With the abnormal influences netted out and only normal market forces prevailing, shadow prices are current normalized prices, rather than current actual prices. They are not forecasts. The analyst assumes that these current normalized prices will prevail over the life of the project. Normal net revenues from the plan can then be calculated and projected into the future. Current normalized agricultural prices, therefore, are a specific kind of shadow price. They approximate what agricultural commodity and factor prices will be in the current year under different conditions than those that actually prevail.

Clearly, current policy governing shadow prices for agricultural commodities differs significantly from the policy that determines shadow prices for other goods and services. There are important efficiency reasons for not using current actual agricultural prices for project evaluation.6/ The most important of these efficiency reasons are price variability and the effect of Government policy on prices.

Farm prices fluctuate in the short term for a number of fairly obvious reasons. First, they vary seasonally, reflecting the cost of storing inventories of food and fiber. However, this is a fairly minor concern, and the use of a season average or annual average price eliminates this source of variability. Second, farm prices are greatly affected on the supply side by variable weather. Third, sudden and unpredictable shifts in foreign demand have a large impact on prices. Using a seasonal or annual average price will not compensate for the latter two sources of variability.

The use of current actual agricultural prices in evaluating resource plans would incorporate such short-term factors into plans designed to operate for 50 to 100 years. These short-term influences would then receive excessive weight in determining the economic viability of resource plans. The set of viable resource plans would therefore include an inappropriately large number of plans that will show a given level of net returns for the year in which the plan was evaluated, but which could be reasonably expected to yield different net returns over a longer period of time.

6/ This is true to some extent for other sectors of the economy as well, but these other considerations are not recognized by current policy. For example, shadow prices should ideally correct for any biases in resource allocation due to monopoly power exercised in certain industries.

For example, consider a hypothetical year in which the Corn Belt suffered from severe drought, world fertilizer supplies were drastically curtailed, and the European Economic Community, the Soviet Union, China, and Japan doubled their import orders for U.S. commodities. The use of actual prices for such a year would significantly overestimate the returns to investment in irrigated agriculture in the Southwest. It is important, therefore, to adjust actual prices to lessen the year-to-year fluctuations, and thereby reduce the probability of serious distortions in resource allocation.

Government policy likewise has a significant short-term influence on agricultural prices. Policies such as the use of a loan rate, or other effective price support, prevent prices from falling below specified levels. Similarly, a price ceiling would influence prices by preventing their rise above a specified level. Acreage allotments and set-aside programs affect prices indirectly by influencing the quantities of resources used in food and fiber production.

The use of current actual prices will institutionalize the effects of Government programs. For a price support program, the use of current actual prices builds into the project a liability for future transfer payments from the Government to producers. In the case of a price ceiling, the use of prevailing prices commits the Government to a policy of excess demand and nonprice rationing in the relevant markets. The appropriate shadow price, in this instance, is an estimate of the market price that would prevail under normal supply and demand conditions, without the influence of Government policies in agricultural markets.[7]

CHARACTERISTICS OF NORMALIZING PROCEDURES

The preceding analysis of the relationships between actual, normalized, and shadow prices should clarify the meaning of normalized prices. For the analyst interested in empirical applications, the next step is to consider how normalized prices can be estimated.

An ideal normalizing procedure should meet several criteria. First and most important, it should yield estimates of normalized prices consistent with the concepts of normalized and shadow prices. Two considerations are important in this regard. In the first place, netting out the effects of short-term supply and demand fluctuations on actual prices should yield normalized price estimates that vary less widely than actual prices. That is, one may reasonably expect a time series of normalized commodity prices to be a smooth version of the corresponding actual prices. Normalized prices should be dampened images of actual prices. The effect of Government programs on actual prices should be reflected in the estimated normalized prices for given supply and demand conditions. For example, a commodity price supported by Government policy should exceed the estimated normalized price once the effect of the Government policy is subtracted out.

Second, it should provide a framework for incorporating all relevant information in the process of estimating normalized prices. Variable demand and supply conditions, as well as Government programs, affect market prices of food and fiber. An ideal normalizing procedure would provide a framework for explicitly including the effects of these factors on prices.

Third, an ideal normalizing procedure should be based on a plausible model of economic

---

[7] This is valid whether or not the Government actually continues its policies in the future. Shadow prices represent the value to society of goods and resources affected by a plan, and not just the actual prices that are likely to be observed.

behavior. Only if this is the case will the procedure have a rational process of assumptions, logic, and conclusions.

Finally, the demands placed on scarce research and analytical resources dictate that an ideal normalizing procedure should be cost effective. The procedure should yield the highest quality estimates for the least possible cost in research time and funds.

The remainder of this report will examine alternative empirical procedures for normalizing prices. These four characteristics will be used as criteria to judge the value of each procedure. Based on this evaluation, the best available procedure for normalizing prices will be presented. Most of the procedures analyzed in this report will not adequately compensate for the effects of Government programs. The discussion that follows therefore focuses on the other criteria presented here.

NORMALIZING PRICES THROUGH TREND ANALYSIS

A Linear Trend Analysis

Prior to 1975, the method used to normalize agricultural commodity and input prices was a straightforward analysis. A linear trend line was fitted to the most recent 10 years of data in a seasonal average price time series for each commodity. The fitted value of the price variable for the most recent year was then taken as the estimated normalized price for that year. The following year, more data in the time series became available and were added to the 10-year sample, while the earliest data of the set were dropped. The normalized price was again taken from the fitted trend line for the most recent year, and a normalized price time series was generated in this fashion.

In actual practice, this procedure was supplemented by judgmental changes in the prices resulting from the procedure. For example, on the basis of:

> Changes in the index of prices received by farmers
> and the index of prices paid by farmers for items
> used in production, . . . all commodity prices were
> adjusted upward by 22.7 percent and all cost items,
> exclusive of labor, were adjusted upward by 12.0
> percent. Labor prices will be the prevailing wage
> rate at the time of plan formation.8/

In a later directive, the following judgmental changes were made:

> In order to more adequately reflect price levels,
> the following criteria were used. . .
>
> 1. The trend price computed from the regression. . .
>   was selected if the trend price was greater
>   than or equal to the previous year's normalized
>   price. . .
> 2. For those commodities in which the trend price
>   was less than the previous year's normalized
>   price, consideration was given to the season
>   average price for the most recent year. . .
>   a. The season average price may be greater

8/ Water Resources Council, Agricultural Price Standards, Washington, D.C., Feb. 1974, p. 3.

than the previous year's normalized price,
in which case the previous year's normalized
price was selected.

b. The season average price could be less than
    or equal to the trend price, in which case
    the trend price was selected.

c. The season average price could be less than
    the previous year's normalized price, but
    greater than the trend price, in which case
    the season average price was used.9/

Clearly, the linear trend procedure was not capable of incorporating enough information to accommodate changing beliefs about normal market conditions and normal prices.
Informed judgment about such changes was applied after the fact, and in a rather ad
hoc manner, because the procedure itself was incapable of incorporating these judgments.

During periods of relatively stable prices, this procedure is adequate. It yields a
price which dampens movements in actual prices without calculating a normalized price
outside the range of recent prices. Figure 1-A (all figures will appear at the end of
this report) displays a series of normalized prices calculated in this fashion for one
principal commodity, wheat, over a period when prices were fairly stable.

When prices fluctuate widely, the linear trend procedure leaves much to be desired.
Several future time paths of prices have been plotted in figures 1-B, 1-C, and 1-D.
Each path of normalized prices was calculated using linear trend procedures.
Alternative one (fig. 1-B) is based on the presumption that wheat prices will return
to their 1974 level and remain there throughout the near future. Note that use of the
linear trend procedure yields normalized prices that are noticeably outside the range
of projected prices for the 1976-78 period. Alternative two (fig. 1-C) assumes that
wheat prices fluctuate erratically around the 1982 level of $2.35 per bushel offi-
cially forecast by the U.S. Department of Agriculture (USDA) in September 1977. In
this case, the procedure hardly dampens these fluctuations at all. Rather, normalized
prices rise at a moderate rate lagging behind actual prices, and then remain high long
after actual prices have declined. Furthermore, normalized prices then dip substanti-
ally below the 1982 projected prices that were officially forecast by USDA in September 1977 (fig. 1-D, alternative three). Normalized prices under these conditions
remain high for 5 years after actual or projected prices have fallen, and again dip
below the projected 1982 price significantly.

The value of a normalizing procedure is the validity of the model of economic behavior
upon which the procedure is founded. This study has not been able to discover any
model of behavior that yields the linear trend approach as a normalizing procedure.

The chief advantage of the linear trend approach is its low cost. It is a simple and
inexpensive matter to calculate normalized prices in this fashion. However, as noted
above, the estimates are likely to be of questionable value. The overall cost effectiveness of this technique is, therefore, also in doubt.

On all four standards, the linear trend procedure is of little value. The approach
does not incorporate enough information; it has no behavioral model as its foundation;
it does not adequately dampen price fluctuations; and while its cost is low, so is its
effectiveness.

9/ Water Resources Council, Agricultural Price Standards, Washington, D.C., Oct.
1974, pp. 3-4.

A Zero-one Shift Method

One alternative to the linear trend approach is the use of a dummy or zero-one shift variable in the regression equation. This procedure is identical to the linear trend approach except that the regression equation includes one more variable besides the time trend. This variable is a dummy variable, with a value of zero assigned to all years prior to the occurrence of a presumed structural shift or change in normal conditions, and a value of one assigned to every year following the change.

For the purpose of this evaluation, the dummy variable was assigned the value of zero for all years prior to 1973. All years from 1973 on are assigned the value of one. This is based on the premise that 1973 marked the beginning of a transition from low-demand and low-input cost conditions to high-demand and high-input cost conditions for U.S. agriculture.

The capability of the zero-one shift approach to incorporate relevant information is clearly superior to that of the linear trend. The dummy variable may remain equal to one as long as the structural factors that necessitated the shift are still in effect. It may then be reset to zero when the conditions that originally necessitated the consideration of a structural shift are no longer present. Furthermore, the number of dummy variables may be expanded to accommodate structural shifts of different types—one variable for changed-demand conditions and a second for changed-input price conditions. In addition, it may be hypothesized that structural shifts may occur in different years for each commodity. Finally, the dummy variable may take on values between zero and one as judgment dictates, thereby introducing an additional dimension of flexibility.

The dampening characteristics of the zero-one shift represent an improvement over the linear trend technique, but are still not completely satisfactory. For purposes of simplicity, only one structural shift variable, equal to zero through 1972 and one afterwards, is displayed in figure 2. During the period of stable prices, 1963-1972 (fig. 2-A), the procedure yields prices identical to those resulting from the linear trend procedure, since the zero-one shift variable was assigned the value zero for each year.10/ In figure 2-B, the time path of normalized prices is very similar to the linear trend method, except that normalized prices respond better to changes in actual prices under the zero-one approach. Under alternatives two and three, the zero-one shift yields time paths that respond better than the linear trend paths, although there is still a noticeable tendency for normalized prices to fall significantly below projected prices from 1979-82.

No model of economic behavior implies the use of the zero-one shift technique. Thus, it cannot be considered to be of any greater value than the linear trend procedure. The zero-one shift approach, like the simple trend analysis, is low in cost, and since it results in slightly more plausible estimates, should be considered marginally more cost effective than the linear trend method.

The zero-one shift, therefore, represents a substantial improvement over the linear trend method in terms of its capability to incorporate information, a partial improvement in terms of its dampening characteristics and overall cost effectiveness, and no improvement at all in its conceptual foundation.

10/ More precisely, the zero-one shift cannot be estimated over this period because the constant term and dummy variable are perfectly multicollinear. By definition, however, the zero-one shift and linear trend techniques must be equivalent.

Extended Time Series Trend Analysis

The linear trend and zero-one shift techniques were analyzed on a longer time series (up to 25 years) with generally discouraging results. In terms of the four basic criteria enumerated, extending the time series yielded no improvement in the results of the linear trend approach. In terms of its ability to incorporate relevant information, the linear trend over the longer time period rates no better than the same analysis over a shorter period. The zero-one shift technique is considerably more flexible over either time period, as discussed earlier.

Over a longer time period, the linear trend and zero-one shift techniques dampen virtually all fluctuations in recent seasonal average prices. The linear trend and zero-one shift approaches assign an equal weight to each year in the time series. As the number of observations increase, each year receives successively less weight. As a result, the estimated normalized price is highly unresponsive to price changes in recent years.

It is quite likely that such highly dampened normalized prices distort the project evaluation. The objective of a normalizing procedure is to exclude those price changes that are due to abnormal fluctuations in market conditions, while incorporating those price changes that are due to changes in normal conditions. To use a normalizing method that is almost entirely unresponsive to current price changes may exclude virtually all changes in normal market conditions. Overdampening the actual price series is just as inappropriate as underdampening it. Either will lead to the distortions in resource allocation that price normalization was designed to preclude. Furthermore, this approach provides no basis for determining how much dampening of fluctuations is desirable.

Extending the time series does not alter the fact that there is no behavior model that implies the use of the trend or zero-one shift approaches. The extended-time series approach costs virtually the same as the shorter time series; the poorer quality of the estimates, however, implies an overall unfavorable cost effectiveness.

WEIGHTED AVERAGE TECHNIQUES FOR NORMALIZING PRICES

A second class of techniques for estimating normalized prices involves using weighted averages of current and past actual prices. In its simplest form, this procedure uses simple averages over a 3- or 5-year period; alternatively, different weights can be assigned to different years in the period. A weighted average approach will meet the fluctuation-dampening requirement established above, while still being responsive to current year price changes. In addition, a particular type of weight pattern can be shown to result from a simple, empirically viable model of price-normalizing behavior, thereby satisfying the criterion that the normalizing procedure has a conceptual foundation in some model of economic behavior.

A Model of Price-normalizing Behavior

This simple model is the following:

$$P_t = P_t^n + u_t \tag{1}$$

where P_t is the observed price at time t; P_t^n is the normal price in time t that would have been observed if market conditions had been normal; and u_t is the short-term

8

fluctuation component of observed price. As time passes and prices change, it is likely that some part of any change in price is due to changes in normal conditions, while the remainder of the price change is transitory. This implies that the process of normalizing prices should include some fraction of the difference between the current actual price and the previous normal price. Algebraically, this is expressed as:

$$P_t^n = P_{t-1}^n + \lambda (P_t - P_{t-1}^n) \tag{2}$$

where λ (lambda) is a real number between zero and one, exclusive.

Now it can be shown (see appendix) that equation 2 is equivalent to

$$P_t^n = \lambda P_t + \lambda(1-\lambda)P_{t-1} + \lambda(1-\lambda)^2 P_{t-2} + \ldots \tag{3}$$

The normal price in each period is simply a weighted average of all previous actual prices, where weight distribution is identified by one parameter, λ. This weight distribution, known as a Koyck [11]/ distribution, is a descending series of weights, such that each successive earlier price contributes less to the current normal price than does each more recent price. The series is infinite and has a sum of unity. This presents no practical problem since the series may be truncated when it approaches sufficiently close to one.

The empirical implementation of this model requires that an estimate of the parameter λ be obtained. Such an estimation is impossible using ordinary least squares regression techniques, as the normalized price in each period is not an observable variable. Two methods for circumventing that problem are the polynomial-distributed lag and the generalized-distributed lag.

Estimating Weights Using a Polynomial Distributed Lag

Using polynomial-distributed lag, one can directly estimate the weight coefficients, rather than the parameter λ, from the price time series for each commodity. Equation 3 can be rewritten as

$$P_t^n = w_o P_t + w_1 P_{t-1} + w_2 P_{t-2} + \ldots \tag{4}$$

It is possible to obtain biased estimates of the w_i individually by estimating a misspecified form of equation 1. This misspecification takes two forms.

First, the infinite series is truncated after 6 years. The equation then becomes:

$$P_t^n = w_o P_t + w_1 P_{t-1} + w_2 P_{t-2} + w_3 P_{t-3} + w_4 P_{t-4} + w_5 P_{t-5} + w_6 P_{t-6} + e_t \tag{5}$$

where e_t is a small, positive error term with a random component (assumed normally distributed with a mean of zero and standard variance) and a small positive component consisting of:

$$w_7 P_{t-7} + w_8 P_{t-8} + \ldots$$

11/ L. M. Koyck, Distributed Lags and Investment Analysis, Amsterdam: North-Holland, 1954.

Second, because the normal price variable is not observable, it is absorbed into the error term. Equation 5 is then transformed into:

$$P_t = - (w_1/w_o)P_{t-1} - (w_2/w_o)P_{t-2} - (w_3/w_o)P_{t-3} - (w_4/w_o)P_{t-4} - (w_5/w_o)P_{t-5} -$$

$$(w_6/w_o)P_{t-6} + (1/w_o)P_t - (e_t/w_o). \tag{6}$$

which is equivalent to:

$$P_t = z_1 P_{t-1} + z_2 P_{t-2} + z_3 P_{t-3} + z_4 P_{t-4} + z_5 P_{t-5} + z_6 P_{t-6} + v_t \tag{7}$$

A direct estimate of equation 7 is then desired. From equation 6, it follows that the w_i has a monotonically decreasing pattern from the current year to earlier years. That is, w_o should be greater than w_1, which should be greater than w_2, and so forth. Furthermore, the w_i should fall in the positive unit interval, and their sum should be one.

By dividing this set of weights by the negative of the largest element in the set, the coefficients of the P_{t-i} in equation 7 become negative, monotonically increasing, and larger in absolute value. The a priori restrictions on the shape of the lag distribution should reflect this expectation, except for one consideration. Since P_t^n is not observable, a regression equation that contains only the other six price terms on the right side will give biased results due to the omitted variable P_t^n.

The technique used in estimating equation 7 is the Almon polynomial distributed-lag method, with the data in logarithmic form and adjusted to compensate for serially correlated errors.[12] Using this technique, it is possible to specify only that the lag coefficients lie in the range of a polynomial of degree n, and that the coefficients approach zero over time. A second degree polynomial was chosen, because this would permit the lag pattern to be monotonic without requiring linearity. The original price-normalizing model implies a geometric, rather than a linear, pattern for the lag coefficients. The coefficients were constrained to approach zero after the 6th year. The coefficients were estimated over the period 1950-76 [13] and are displayed in table 1.

Of the 54 commodity and input prices and price indices that were analyzed in this manner, 45 yielded estimated weight distributions that were monotonically decreasing.[14] An additional seven price series resulted in distributions that decreased over the first 4 or 5 lag years, and increased afterwards. Only two commodities, grapefruit and potatoes, yielded distributions that first increased, and then decreased.

These results suggested that the bias of the coefficients of equation 7 from the omission of the variable P_t^n is substantial. It is great enough to prevent the expected weight pattern for z_i from appearing.

12/ S. Almon, "The Distributed Lag Between Capital Appropriations and Expenditures," Econometrica, Vol. 33, No. 1 (Jan. 1965), 178-98; C. Cochrane and C. Orcutt, "Application of Least-Squares Regressions to Relationships Containing Auto-correlated Error Terms," Journal of American Statistical Association, Vol. 44 (1949), 32-61.

13/ The data are described more fully in R. Niehaus, "Data and Procedures for Calculating 1975 Normalized Agricultural Prices for the U.S. Water Resources Council," Unpublished manuscript, Economics, Statistics, and Cooperatives Service, U.S. Department of Agriculture, Washington, D.C.

14/ The equations for several input price indices were estimated with only 4 lag years. Data were available for these series only for the period 1965-76, and this did not permit enough degrees of freedom to estimate 6 lag years.

Table 1--Almon's polynomial distributed lag results using equation 7

Commodities	z_{t-1}	z_{t-2}	z_{t-3}	z_{t-4}	z_{t-5}	z_{t-6}
Wheat, all 1/	0.232	-0.025	-0.198	-0.281	-0.276	-0.182
Rye 1/	.018	-.255	-.421	-.478	-.427	-.268
Rice	.343	.258	.184	.121	.069	.029
Corn for grain 1/	.137	-.016	-.117	.165	-.162	.107
Oats 1/	.374	.177	.034	.055	-.091	-.072
Barley 1/	.529	.158	-.099	-.244	-.276	-.194
Sorghum grain	.430	.288	.174	.088	.030	.001
Hay, all 1/	.736	.390	.134	-.033	-.112	-.101
Dry edible beans	.376	.275	.189	.118	.063	.023
Sugarbeets	.253	.232	.203	.165	.118	.063
Sugarcane	.300	.250	.199	.149	.099	.049
Cotton lint 1/	.611	.338	.134	-.002	-.070	-.069
Tobacco	.353	.236	.142	.071	.024	0
Cottonseed	.379	.272	.183	.112	.057	.020
Soybeans	.387	.295	.214	.144	.085	.036
Peanuts	.566	.328	.147	.024	-.041	-.049
Flaxseed	.343	.267	.199	.138	.084	.039
Apples	.410	.273	.164	.081	.027	0
Oranges	.594	.339	.146	.016	-.051	-.057
Grapefruit 2/	.229	.236	.224	.195	.148	.083
Potatoes 2/	.173	.225	.244	.232	.187	.110
Sweet potatoes	.384	.278	.189	.117	.061	.022
Steers and heifers	.398	.278	.179	.102	.046	.012
Feeder steers, eight markets	.386	.274	.181	.108	.053	.017
Cows for slaughter	.308	.249	.193	.140	.090	.043
Calves	.355	.264	.187	.121	.068	.028
Sheep	.243	.233	.210	.176	.129	.070
Lambs	.455	.298	.174	.081	.021	.005
Hogs	.454	.299	.175	.084	.024	-.004
Milk	.430	.295	.185	.100	.041	.007
Cream	.355	.245	.156	.086	.037	.008
Broilers	.590	.336	.145	-.016	-.051	-.056
Turkeys	.606	.341	.142	.008	-.060	-.062
Eggs	.578	.329	.141	.015	-.051	-.056
Wool	.276	.224	.174	.127	.082	.039
Prices received, all farm production	.436	.290	.173	.086	.028	-.001
Prices received, all crops	.418	.284	.176	.093	.037	.005
Prices received, livestock production	.453	.295	.171	.079	.019	-.006
Prices paid, items used in production	.434	.290	.174	.086	.029	0
Feed	.423	.286	.175	.091	.034	.004
Feeder livestock	.478	.303	.166	.067	.007	-.015
Seed	.424	.287	.177	.093	.035	.004
Fertilizer	.420	.284	.175	.091	.035	.004
Agricultural chemicals	.950	.305	-.068	-.170	0	0
Fuels and energy	.532	.310	.148	.044	0	0
Farm and motor supplies	.436	.308	.193	.091	0	0
Autos and trucks	.426	.313	.205	.100	0	0
Tractors and self-propelled machinery	.724	.309	.050	-.053	0	0
Other machinery	.809	.308	.006	-.096	0	0
Building and fencing	.497	.312	.167	.063	.002	-.020
Wage rates	.438	.292	.176	.088	.030	0
Construction costs composite index	.434	.290	.175	.088	.030	.001
ENR construction costs	.438	.292	.176	.088	.030	0
Wholesale lumber price index	.443	.293	.174	.084	.026	-.002

1/ A weight distribution that first declines, then rises in the fifth or sixth lag year.
2/ A weight distribution that first increases, then decreases.

11

However, the results do not significantly differ from expectations for the w_i of equation 4. The procedure that will be followed uses the estimated coefficients of equation 7 as first approximations for the coefficients of equation 4.

In order to do this, it is necessary to adjust the estimated coefficients displayed in table 1. It will be required that the w_i be a value between zero and one inclusive, with a sum of one. Consequently, the weight coefficients for each commodity are increased or decreased by the amount of the absolute value of the smallest coefficient. In effect, the whole distribution shifts up or down so the minimum coefficient is zero. Any coefficient for an earlier year is set equal to zero as well, and the remaining (positive) weights are adjusted proportionately, summing to one (displayed in table 2).

In general, the weighted average with directly estimated weights dampens fluctuations in actual prices while still bearing some resemblance to the actual price time series (fig. 3). This is particularly noticeable for alternative two. Unlike the other two methods, there is no tendency to fall below actual or projected prices under alternatives two and three. In addition, normalized prices are more responsive to actual price declines than they were for the linear trend and zero-one shift methods under alternatives two and three. As a method for dampening fluctuations, the polynomial distributed-lag approach is a definite improvement over the linear-trend and zero-one shift models. In addition, the distributed lag is founded on a model of economic behavior, which is not the case for the other techniques. The distributed-lag method costs less, so its cost effectiveness is significantly greater than the other approaches.

The polynomial distributed-lag estimation procedure provides little room for incorporating necessary information about changes in normal market conditions. In this respect, it is no improvement over the linear trend and is not as desirable as the zero-one shift. The estimation process is fairly complex. Direct estimation is possible only by misspecifying the model. By directly estimating the weights, it is not possible to obtain a unique estimate of λ from each regression. Thus, the estimated weights are an approximation of the weight series in the model, rather than a statistically unbiased estimate of the parameter λ.

On the whole, however, the polynomial distributed-lag approach is a significant improvement over the linear trend. The polynomial lag procedure is used by the USDA to calculate the normalized prices published by the WRC (see appendix table 1). Commodity group averages of these weights are displayed in table 3.

This analysis is carried out for U.S. average prices. These U.S. prices, in turn, are used to calculate State-level normalized prices. The State prices are derived by adjusting the U.S. average price upward or downward by the average ratio of the State price to the U.S. price for the most recent 3 years.[15]

Estimating Weights Using a Generalized Distributed Lag

A second approach to determining the weight distribution is to specify an a priori value of λ for each commodity based on the judgment of persons familiar with that commodity market. The primary advantage of this approach is that it permits normalized prices to be as responsive as one desires to the movement of actual prices. A disadvantage is that it allows more room for individuals to disagree or to introduce their own biases. A value of λ close to one yields a highly responsive normalized price; a value of λ close to zero yields a less responsive normalized price.

Table 4 displays several illustrative weight series for different values of the Koyck

[15] Agricultural Price Standards, pp. 15-18.

Table 2--Polynomial distribution lag regression results using equation 4

Commodities	w_t	w_{t-1}	w_{t-2}	w_{t-3}	w_{t-4}
Wheat, all	0.603	0.300	0.097	0.0	0.0
Rye	.639	.287	.073	0	0
Rice	.378	.276	.187	.111	.048
Corn for grain	.605	.299	.096	0	0
Oats	.520	.300	.140	.040	0
Barley	.556	.300	.122	.022	0
Sorghum grain	.427	.286	.172	.087	0.029
Hay, all	.506	.300	.147	.047	0
Dry edible beans	.390	.278	.183	.105	.044
Sugarbeets	.290	.258	.213	.155	.084
Sugarcane	.334	.267	.199	.133	.066
Cotton lint	.500	.300	.150	.050	0
Tobacco	.427	.286	.172	.086	.029
Cottonseed	.398	.279	.181	.102	.041
Soybeans	.371	.274	.188	.114	.052
Peanuts	.485	.297	.154	.058	.006
Flaxseed	.364	.273	.191	.118	.054
Apples	.429	.286	.172	.085	.028
Oranges	.490	.298	.153	.055	.005
Grapefruit	.237	.248	.229	.182	.105
Potatoes	.123	.225	.262	.239	.151
Sweet potatoes	.394	.279	.182	.103	.042
Steers and heifers	.409	.282	.177	.095	.036
Feeder steers, eight markets	.402	.280	.179	.099	.039
Cows for slaughter	.346	.269	.196	.127	.061
Calves	.382	.276	.186	.109	.047
Sheep	.270	.254	.218	.165	.092
Lambs	.448	.292	.168	.076	.016
Hogs	.434	.287	.170	.083	.027
Milk	.416	.283	.175	.092	.033
Cream	.414	.282	.176	.093	.035
Broilers	.503	.305	.157	.031	.004
Turkeys	.496	.299	.151	.052	.001
Eggs	.491	.298	.152	.055	.004
Wool	.344	.269	.196	.128	.063
Prices received, all farm products	.429	.286	.171	.085	.028
Prices received, all crops	.420	.284	.174	.090	.033
Prices received, livestock production	.438	.287	.169	.081	.024
Prices paid, items used in production	.428	.286	.172	.086	.029
Feed	.424	.285	.173	.088	.030
Feeder livestock	.450	.290	.165	.075	.020
Seed	.422	.284	.174	.089	.031
Fertilizer	.422	.284	.174	.088	.031
Agricultural chemicals	.660	.280	.060	0	0
Fuels and energy	.515	.300	.143	.043	0
Farm and motor supplies	.424	.300	.188	.089	0
Autos and trucks	.408	.300	.196	.096	0
Tractors and self-propelled machinery	.626	.291	.083	0	0
Other machinery	.641	.286	.072	0	0
Building and fencing	.453	.291	.164	.073	.019
Wages rates	.428	.285	.172	.086	.029
Construction costs, composite index	.428	.286	.172	.086	.029
ENR construction costs index	.428	.285	.172	.086	.029
Wholesale lumber price index	.432	.286	.171	.083	.027

Table 3--Estimated averaged weights by commodity

Item	:	w_t	:	w_{t-1}	:	w_{t-2}	:	w_{t-3}	:	w_{t-4}
Grains 1/	:	0.533		0.293		0.127		0.037		0.011
Fruits 2/	:	.385		.277		.185		.107		.046
Vegetables 3/	:	.353		.270		.194		.124		.059
Other crops 4/	:	.396		.279		.181		.102		.042
Livestock products 5/	:	.385		.283		.177		.093		.035
Inputs 6/	:	.489		.290		.147		.061		.013

1/ Wheat, rye, rice, corn, oats, barley, sorghum.
2/ Apples, oranges, grapefruit.
3/ Dry beans, potatoes, sweet potatoes.
4/ Cottonseed, soybeans, peanuts, flaxseed, tobacco cotton, sugarbeets, sugarcane, hay.
5/ Steers and heifers, feeder steers (eight market average), cows for slaughter, calves, sheep, lambs, hogs, milk, cream, broilers, turkeys, eggs, wool.
6/ Feed, feeder livestock, seed, fertilizer, agricultural chemicals, fuels and energy, farm and motor supplies, autos and trucks, tractors and self-propelled machinery, other machinery, building and fencing, wage rates.

parameter λ , generated using equation 3. For $\lambda = 0.5$, (the dashed line of figure 4) the calculated series is very close to the series computed from the directly estimated weights. The use of the predetermined weight scheme possesses the same advantages over the linear trend and zero-one shift approaches mentioned above; it does not over-shoot actual prices under alternative one, and it is responsive to declines in actual prices under alternatives two and three.

Both weighted average methods represent significant improvements over linear trend techniques in several ways. First, the generalized and polynomial approaches dampen processes under all possible time paths of actual prices. Second, both result from a conceptual model of price-normalizing behavior. There are problems in the empirical application of this model, but the errors introduced in solving these problems are probably within the margin of error of the project evaluation process as a whole. Third, the generalized approach (a priori specification of λ) is flexible enough to take into account changing judgments about what are normal market conditions. At the same time, of course, this flexibility permits errors and individual biases in judgments to receive more emphasis in normalizing prices. Finally, both approaches are cost effective.

THE STRUCTURAL APPROACH TO NORMALIZED PRICES

The final normalizing procedure to be considered uses structural models of agricultural markets to estimate normalized prices. This approach has not yet been attempted,

Table 4—Sample weight distributions for given values of the adaptation parameter

Lag year	Value of: λ				
	0.6	0.5	0.4	0.3	0.2
	0.600	0.500	0.400	0.300	0.200
	1/ .600	1/ .500	1/ .400	1/ .300	1/ .200
t-1	.240	.250	.240	.210	.160
	1/ .840	1/ .750	1/ .640	1/ .510	1/ .360
t-2	.096	.125	.144	.147	.128
	1/ .936	1/ .875	1/ .784	1/ .657	1/ .488
t-3	.038	.063	.086	.103	.102
	1/ .974	1/ .938	1/ .870	1/ .760	1/ .590
t-4	.015	.031	.052	.072	.082
	1/ .990	1/ .969	1/ .922	1/ .832	1/ .672
t-5	--	.016	.031	.050	.066
	--	1/ .984	1/ .953	1/ .882	1/ .738
t-6	--	.008	.019	.035	.052
	--	1/ .992	1/ .972	1/ .918	1/ .790
t-7	--	--	.011	.025	.042
	--	--	1/ .983	1/ .942	1/ .832
t-8	--	--	.007	.017	.034
	--	--	1/ .990	1/ .960	1/ .866

1/ Cumulative proportions of the total distributions.
  -- = Not applicable.

so it will be discussed in very general terms.

Such models of the agricultural sector include supply and demand equations for food and fiber products and for agricultural inputs. The agricultural models can then determine the prices and quantities of the commodities and inputs involved for given levels of technology, consumer preferences, market structure, and for given values of the relevant exogenous variables—population, weather, Government policy, foreign demand, and nonagricultural variables.

In this framework, current normalized prices could be calculated by specifying a current normal value for each exogenous variable, then solving the model for the current values of the endogenous prices. These prices would be the normalized prices associated with current normal market conditions. The difference between the normalized prices and the actual observed prices would represent the abnormal component of actual prices in the given year.

This procedure has several advantages. First, it clearly possesses the capability of incorporating relevant information directly into the price-normalizing process. This is particularly important when Government policy plays a large role in setting agricultural prices. The weighted-average approach, described previously, is adequate when the primary concern in normalizing prices is the smoothing or dampening of market fluctuations. However, the weighted average approach does not readily permit incorporating information about Government policy into the calculation of normalized prices; a different approach is needed. Since U.S. agriculture has reentered a phase of productive abundance, low prices, and active Government intervention, the structural concept described here deserves further consideration.

Second, the structural approach is founded on the theory of market behavior and, therefore, possesses a conceptual basis that can be examined and evaluated.

Third, the normalized price estimates resulting from this procedure would be consistent with the qualitative nature of normalized prices. The primary criterion used to judge a structural model is how well it explains actual behavior and predicts actual prices. It is doubtful that a simple change in the values of exogenous variables would cause an otherwise well-behaved model to deteriorate so badly that its estimates are qualitatively inconsistent with expectations. This is a critical issue, however, requiring further analysis.

The most important questions about this procedure are those of feasibility and cost. Such models do, in fact, exist and a number of proprietary models are available, in addition to those developed in the Government, universities, and other institutions. Although models may not be available for the 54 commodities and inputs analyzed in this report, commodities and inputs of principal interest to project analysts and planners are presently covered.

The cost of adapting and using this model is less certain. There are probably significant initial costs to acquire and modify existing models. After that, the costs of periodically updating data and reestimating normalizing prices will probably be minimal. Thus, the structural approach described here may be potentially the most satisfactory procedure for estimating normalized prices. It deserves further study.

CONCLUSIONS AND RECOMMENDATIONS

Normalized agricultural prices are particular kinds of shadow prices. The use of normalized prices in resource planning is justified on the grounds of economic efficiency. The use of current actual prices is more likely to result in an inefficient allocation of public investment resources than is the use of normalized prices.

To calculate these important prices, several techniques are avaliable. The linear trend method of estimating normalized prices was an effective low-cost technique for smoothing price fluctuations as long as the fluctuations were not large. When the changes are large, this technique performs poorly. Furthermore, it is not capable of incorporating information about Government policy or other important variables in any explicit way. Including a zero-one shift variable improved flexibility of the procedure without raising its cost significantly, but the price-smoothing ability of the approach remained basically unchanged. Neither the linear trend nor the zero-one shift method is based on a theory of economic behavior.

The use of a weighted-average approach, where the weights are either directly estimated using a polynomial distributed lag or prespecified as a Koyck distribution, is
a substantial improvement as a price-smoothing process. The cost of the technique is
low, and the procedure is founded on a simple model of price-normalizing behavior.
However, the ability of this procedure to take into account relevant information about
normal market conditions is quite limited. Nevertheless, this approach is a net improvement over the linear trend method and is currently used by USDA to estimate
normalized prices.

As U.S. agriculture enters a period of active Government intervention, the adequacy of
the weighted average approach is less certain. In particular, the use of a normalizing procedure facilitates analyses of Government price policies. The structural
model of the U.S. food and fiber sector offers significant promise in this regard, and
merits further study.

NORMALIZED WHEAT PRICES

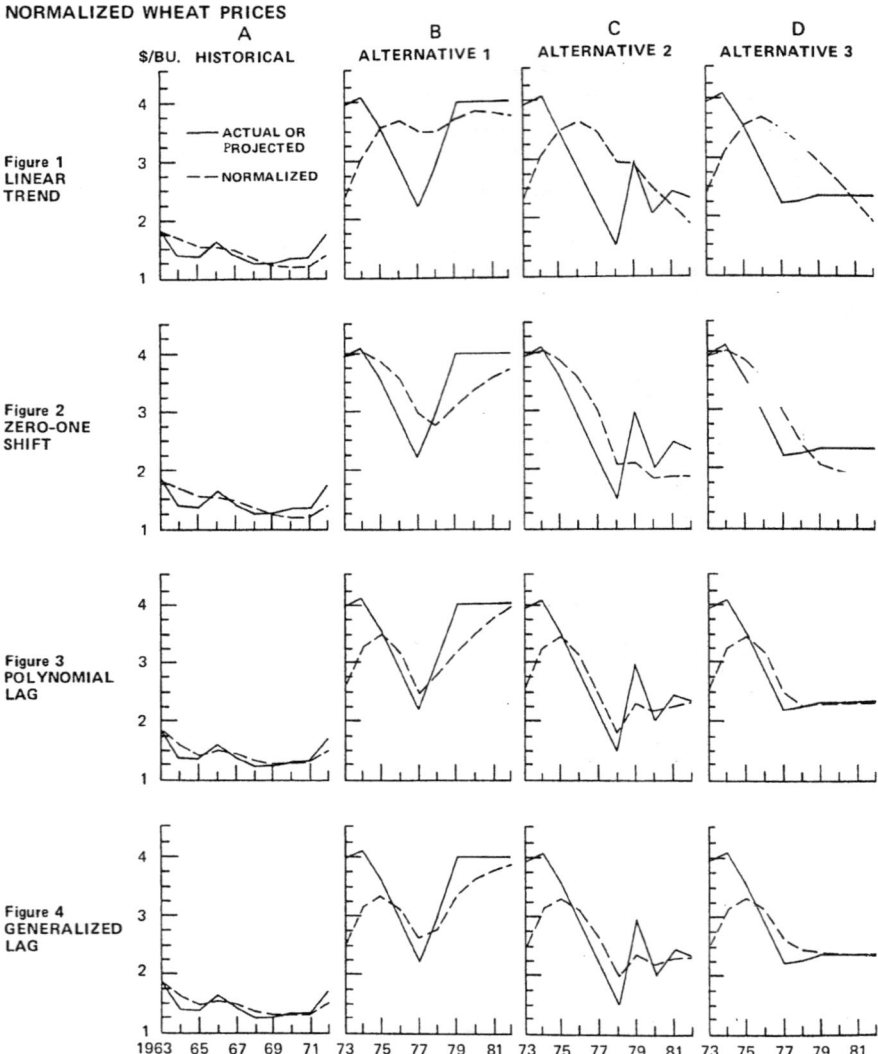

Figure 1 LINEAR TREND

Figure 2 ZERO-ONE SHIFT

Figure 3 POLYNOMIAL LAG

Figure 4 GENERALIZED LAG

A $/BU. HISTORICAL

B ALTERNATIVE 1

C ALTERNATIVE 2

D ALTERNATIVE 3

ACTUAL OR PROJECTED

NORMALIZED

APPENDIX: DERIVATION OF AN INFINITE GEOMETRIC
SERIES FROM AN ADAPTIVE NORMALIZING PROCESS

Let the normalized price of a commodity in time t be equal to the normalized price in time t-1 plus some proportion, λ, of the discrepancy between the observed price in time t and the normal price in t-1.

Repeating equation 2:

$$P_t^n = P_t^n + \lambda(P_t - P_{t-1}^n)$$

Collecting terms on the right-hand side:

$$P_t^n = (1-\lambda)P_{t-1}^n + \lambda P_t$$

Adding $-(1-\lambda)P_{t-1}^n$ to each side, we have:

$$P_t^n - (1-\lambda)P_{t-1}^n = \lambda P_t$$

Next, define a delay operator D such that $DP_t = P_{t-1}$:

We can then write: $D^2 P_t = P_{t-2}, \ldots$

$$P_t^n - \lambda(1-\lambda)DP_t^n = \lambda P_t$$

Again collecting terms,

$$P_t^n (1-(1-\lambda)D) = \lambda P_t$$

Multiplying both sides by $1/(1-(1-\lambda)D)$, we obtain:

$$P_t^n = \frac{\lambda}{1-(1-\lambda)D} P_t$$

which expresses each period's normal price as a function of actual prices. Note that the expression $1/(1-(1-\lambda)D)$ is the sum of the infinite geometric series:

$$1 + (1-\lambda)D + (1-\lambda)^2 D^2 + (1-\lambda)^3 D^3 + \ldots = \sum_{i=0}^{\infty} \lambda^i D^i.$$

By substitution into equation 2, we then have:

or:

$$P_t^n = \lambda \sum_{i=0}^{\infty} (1-\lambda)^i D^i P_t$$

$$P_t^n = \lambda P_t + \lambda(1-\lambda)P_{t-1} + \lambda(1-\lambda)^2 P_{t-2} + \lambda(1-\lambda)^3 P_{t-3} + \ldots \quad (3)$$

The result, then, is that the formulation of normalized prices according to equation implies that each period's normal price is a weighted average of current and all past actual prices. These weights are an infinite geometric series whose sum is one.[1]

---

[1] J. Johnston, _Econometric Methods_, 2nd ed. New York: McGraw-Hill Publishing Co., 1972, chapter 10.

19

Appendix Table 1--Prices received by farmers for principal commodities and August 1977 normalized prices

Commodity	Unit	1972	1973	1974	1975	1976 1/	August 1977
Season Average Prices				Dollars			
Food grains:							
Wheat, all 2/	Bu.	1.76	3.95	4.09	3.52	2.85	3.15
Rye 2/	Bu.	.96	1.91	2.51	2.34	2.36	2.40
Rice 2/	Cwt.	6.73	13.80	11.20	7.93	6.63	8.46
Feed grains and hay:							
Corn for grain 2/	Bu.	1.57	2.55	3.03	2.46	2.32	2.45
Oats 2/	Bu.	.72	1.18	1.53	1.44	1.55	1.50
Barley 2/	Bu.	1.21	2.13	2.80	2.42	2.29	2.39
Sorghum grain 2/	Cwt.	2.45	3.82	4.96	4.21	3.70	4.01
Hay, all (baled)	Ton	31.30	41.60	50.90	53.00	60.40	55.33
Dry beans	Cwt.	11.00	27.30	20.00	21.80	15.40	18.20
Sugarbeets 3/	Ton	16.00	29.60	46.80	27.40	19.80	27.10
Sugarcane for sugar 3/	Ton	11.70	20.90	48.50	20.80	13.40	20.16
Cotton, lint (upland) 4/	Lb.	.273	.446	.501	.429	.650	.558
Tobacco	Lb.	.830	.901	1.086	1.021	1.125	1.059
Oil-bearing crops:							
Cottonseed	Ton	49.50	100.10	135.50	97.50	103.00	102.98
Soybeans for beans	Bu.	4.37	5.69	6.64	4.60	7.32	6.10
Peanuts harvested for nuts	Lb.	.145	.162	.179	.196	.200	.193
Flaxseed	Bu.	3.10	7.56	9.66	6.52	7.03	7.08
Fruits:							
Apples, commercial crop 5/	Lb.	.064	.088	.084	.078	.088	.079
Oranges, all 6/	Box	2.87	2.69	2.78	2.69	2.78	2.77
Grapefruit, all 6/	Box	2.89	2.70	2.41	2.60	2.14	2.46
Vegetables:							
Potatoes	Cwt.	3.01	4.92	4.00	4.80	3.36	4.04
Sweet potatoes	Cwt.	5.75	7.30	7.75	9.13	7.08	7.45
Average Annual Prices							
Livestock:							
Steers and heifers	Cwt.	35.60	45.30	38.30	36.30	36.50	37.49
Feeder steers, eight markets	Cwt.	37.55	48.40	36.75	32.00	37.08	36.49
Cows for slaughter	Cwt.	24.40	32.00	24.80	19.80	24.50	23.98
Calves	Cwt.	44.70	56.60	35.20	27.20	34.10	34.49
Sheep	Cwt.	7.28	12.90	11.30	11.20	13.20	11.54
Lambs	Cwt.	29.10	35.10	37.00	42.10	46.90	42.40
Hogs	Cwt.	25.10	38.40	34.20	46.10	43.30	41.33
Dairy products:							
Milk 7/	Cwt.	6.07	7.14	8.33	8.71	9.66	8.77
Cream, (fat) 7/	Lb.	.678	.672	.635	.670	.834	.739
Poultry and eggs:							
Broilers, commercial	Lb.	.141	.240	.215	.263	.236	.240
Turkeys	Lb.	.222	.382	.280	.348	.317	.323
Eggs	Doz.	.309	.525	.533	.525	.584	.553
Wool	Lb.	.350	.827	.591	.447	.657	.664

1/ Preliminary
2/ Includes allowance for loans outstanding and purchases by the Government valued at the average loan and purchase rate, by States. Does not include price support payments.
3/ Does not include payments under the Sugar Act.
4/ Prices based on 480-pound net weight bale. 1968-1971 includes allowance for unredeemed loans.
5/ Both fresh and processed sale prices (equivalent packinghouse-door returns for Washington and Oregon, equivalent first delivery point for California and "as sold" for other States).
6/ Equivalent packinghouse-door returns per box for all uses.
7/ Sold to plants and dealers.

Appendix Table 2--Indexes of prices received by farmers, paid by farmers, and for construction cost items with August 1977 normalized indexes

(1967 = 100)

Item	1972	1973	1974	1975	1976 1/	August 1977
Prices received by farmers:						
All farm products	125	179	192	186	186	184
All crops	114	175	224	201	197	197
Livestock and livestock products	136	183	165	172	177	173
Prices paid by farmers for all commodities bought for use in production:						
Feed	121	146	166	182	193	178
Livestock	106	160	194	187	191	184
Seed	149	192	148	134	154	149
Fertilizer	135	167	215	245	241	226
Agricultural chemicals	94	102	167	217	185	177
Farm and motor supplies	103	105	119	160	174	166
Autos and trucks	114	120	147	168	164	157
Tractors and self-prop. machinery	137	145	161	191	212	188
Building and fencing materials	128	137	161	195	217	205
Wage rates for hired farm labor	131	147	181	206	215	199
	142	155	178	192	210	192
Construction costs:						
Composite index (U.S. Dept. Of Commerce)	139	152	173	190	198	185
ENR construction cost	163	177	188	206	224	206
Wholesale lumber price (U.S. Dept. Of Labor)	159	205	207	193	233	212

1/ Preliminary

☆ U S GOVERNMENT PRINTING OFFICE · 1978 280-931/171

STATES DEPARTMENT OF AGRICULTURE
WASHINGTON, D.C. 20250

———————

CPSIA information can be obtained
at www.ICGtesting.com
Printed in the USA
BVHW040727310119
538843BV00016B/368/P

9 780331 398212